Days of the Week

Saturday

by Mary Lindeen • illustrated by Javier González

Content Consultant: Susan Kesselring, M.A., Literacy Educator and Preschool Director

magic wagon

visit us at
www.abdopublishing.com

Printed in the United States.

Text by Mary Lindeen
Illustrations by Javier González
Edited by Patricia Stockland
Interior layout and design by Becky Daum
Cover design by Becky Daum

Library of Congress Cataloging-in-Publication Data

Lindeen, Mary.
  Saturday / Mary Lindeen ; illustrated by Javier A. González ; content consultant, Susan Kesselring.
    p. cm. —— (Days of the week)
  ISBN 978-1-60270-102-1
  I. Days——Juvenile literature. I. González, Javier A., 1974– ill. II. Kesselring, Susan. III. Title.
  GR930.L564 2008
  529'.1——dc22

                                2007034071

Seven days in a week
are always the same.
What comes after Friday?
Do you know its name?

If you said "Saturday,"

then you knew which one.

It's day number seven.

Now this week is done.

No work for most people,

and no school for you.

On the weekend, you choose

what you like to do!

Some people sleep late.

Some people do chores.

Some people go shopping,

and some play outdoors.

Some families use Saturdays

for nice time together.

Some people plant gardens

and hope for good weather.

Saturday for some
is a holy day.
They gather together
to worship and pray.

One Saturday in May
is Armed Forces Day.
We thank these strong people
for being so brave.

There's plenty to do
with your Saturday.
Read books, visit friends,
or put on a play!

When Saturday is over,

the old week is done.

Tomorrow is Sunday.

A new week's begun!

21

The Days of the Week

1 Sunday

2 Monday

3 Tuesday

4 Wednesday

7
Saturday

6
Friday

5
Thursday

SOW-A-SEED SATURDAY

On the next Saturday, have a grown-up help you plant a seed. You can plant a seed in dirt outdoors, or you can "plant" a bean between a moist paper towel and the side of a clear cup. No matter what you plant, you'll have fun watching it grow!

SATURDAY'S SCHEDULE

What do you usually do on Saturday? Write or draw your normal Saturday activities. What would you like to do on Saturday? Now write or draw your idea of the Saturday you'd love to have.

WORDS TO KNOW

chore: the daily work of a house or farm.

holy: devoted to a god.

weekend: the days at the beginning and end of the week; Saturday and Sunday.

worship: to take part in honoring a god.